*Choir -*
**Arranged by**

# Offerings of Praise

**Songs by**

Matt Redman, Reuben Morgan, Keith Green,
Stuart Townend, Lynn DeShazo, Rick Muchow, Kyle Rasmussen,
David Ruis, Kevin Jamieson

**PRODUCTS AVAILABLE**

Choral Book  0-6330-0495-2
Listening Cassette  0-6330-1342-0
Listening CD  0-6330-1343-9
Accompaniment Cassette  0-6330-1388-9
(Side A: Split-track/Side B: Instruments only)
Accompaniment CD (Split-track)  0-6330-1389-7
Orchestration  0-6330-1433-8
Cassette Promo Pak  0-6330-1390-0
CD Promo Pak  0-6330-1391-9

**GENEVOX**

© Copyright 2001 GENEVOX. Nashville, TN 37234.
Possession of a CCLI license does not grant you permission to make copies of this piece of music.
For clarification about the rights CCLI does grant you, please call 1-800-234-2446.

# A Word from J. Daniel Smith

As a minister of music, I know how important it is to have the right resource for leading my congregation in worship. Finding the right material that "speaks" to your own congregation can be a great challenge. Not only does it need to have the right musical elements but, more importantly, the material needs to be saying something that accurately reflects the current condition of the group of believers that you lead.

The material contained within this collection has become a viable expression of praise and worship for my own congregation for the reasons mentioned above; it is musically right for us, and it is saying something we want to express. From the newer, more contemporary tunes to the older hymns that have been given a fresh setting, I pray you will find all of this material to be a wonderful resource for exalting the only One who is worthy to receive our praise and adoration. May your choir and worship leaders be infused with life as they consider these lyrics and find them a fitting and appropriate expression of gratitude to the Savior.

# Contents

At Calvary ............................................. 71

The Father's Song ................................. 95

High and Exalted with Holy Is the Lord ....... 44

How Deep the Father's Love for Us ............ 58

Jesus Paid It All ................................... 35

The King of Love .................................. 20

O Lord, You're Beautiful ........................ 118

We Will Dance ....................................... 5

The Wonders of God ........................... 106

You Are Holy ...................................... 83

# We Will Dance

Words and Music by
DAVID RUIS
*Arranged by J. Daniel Smith*

12
cel - e - bra - tion, Lift up a shout of
C
C sus
C (no 3rd)
C sus
14
praise; For the Bride - groom will come,
C
C sus
F
F ♯4 2
16
the glo - ri - ous One.
F
C (no 3rd)
C sus
18
And oh, we will look on His
C
C2
B♭2
F

face; We'll go to a much better place. So dance with all your might, Lift up your hands and clap for joy; For the time's draw-ing near when He will ap - pear. He will ap -

pear. And oh, we will stand by His side, a strong,

pure spotless bride. And we will dance on the streets that are golden, The glorious bride and the great Son of Man;\_ From ev-'ry\_ tongue and tribe\_\_ and na-tion, We'll join\_\_\_\_ in the song of the\_ Lamb.\_\_\_

F  C  C  B♭  F  C  B♭2  F  C(no 3rd)  C sus  C  C sus

*unis.*  *decresc.*

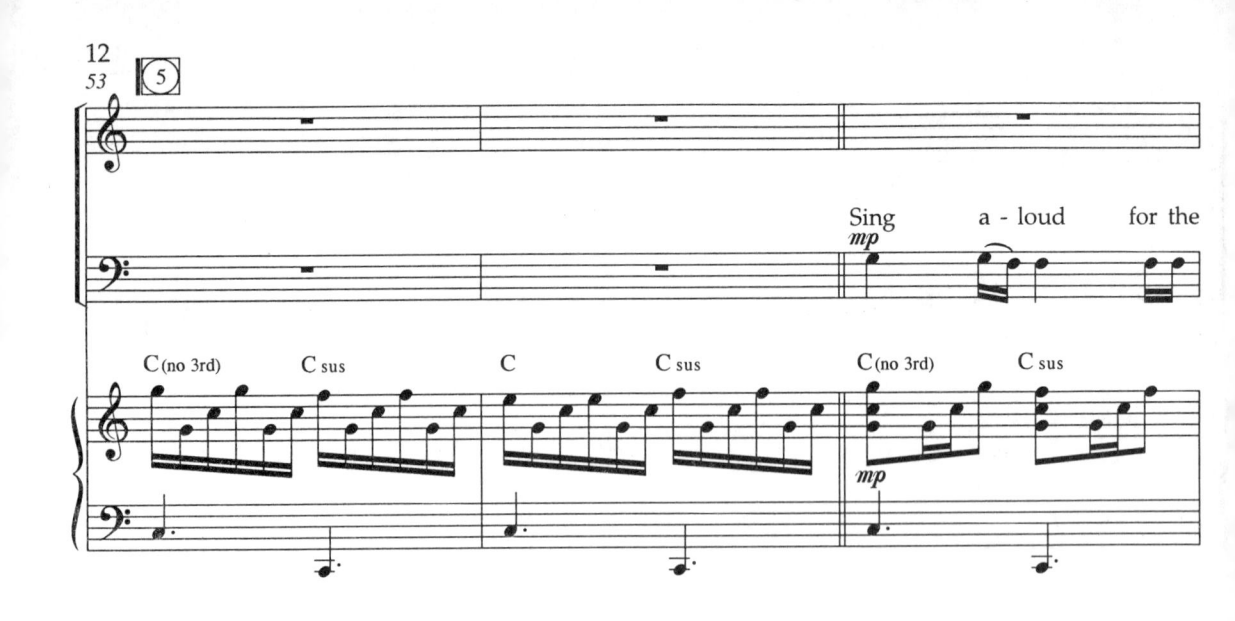

Sing a - loud for the time of re - joic - ing is near; Sing a - loud for the time of re - joic - ing is near; The ris - en King, our

60
The ris - en King, our
Groom, is soon to ap - pear.
C C2 C Csus C Dm/C
62
Groom, is soon to ap - pear.
The wed - ding feast to
C Dm/C C Dm/C C(no 3rd) Csus
64
The wed - ding feast to
come is now near at hand;
C C2 C Csus C Dm/C

come is now near at hand; Lift up your voice, pro-
claim the com-ing Lamb; Lift up your voice, pro-
claim the com-ing Lamb; the

Lamb._____ And we will dance on the streets____ that__ are gold-en, The glo-ri-ous bride and the great Son of Man;___ From ev-'ry__ tongue and tribe and nation, We'll join in the song of the Lamb.

And we will dance on the streets

that are gold-en, The glo-ri-ous bride and the great Son of Man; From ev-'ry tongue and tribe and na-tion, We'll join

unis.
in the song of the_ Lamb._

We'll join_ in the song of the_ Lamb._

We'll join in the song of the Lamb. The song of the Lamb!

# The King of Love

Words and Music by
STUART TOWNEND
and KEVIN JAMIESON
Arranged by J. Daniel Smith

Joyfully (♩ = ca. 130)

21

CHOIR unis.

The King of love is my delight,— His eyes are fire, His face is light;— The First and Last, the Living One,— His name is Jesus.— And from His mouth there comes a sound— That shakes the earth and splits the ground; And yet this voice is life to me, The voice of Je-sus. And I will sing my songs of love, Call-

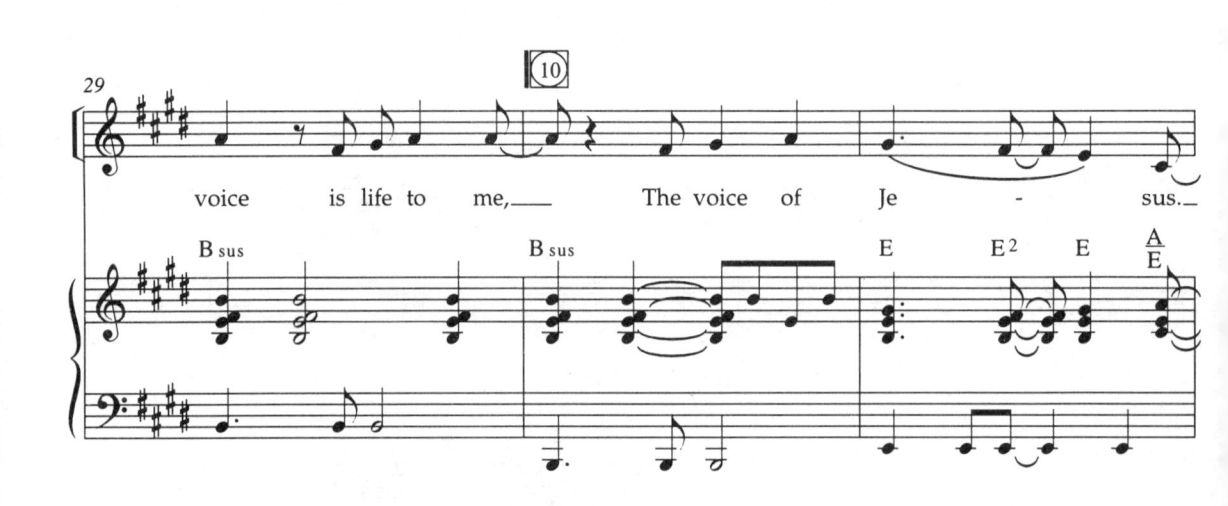

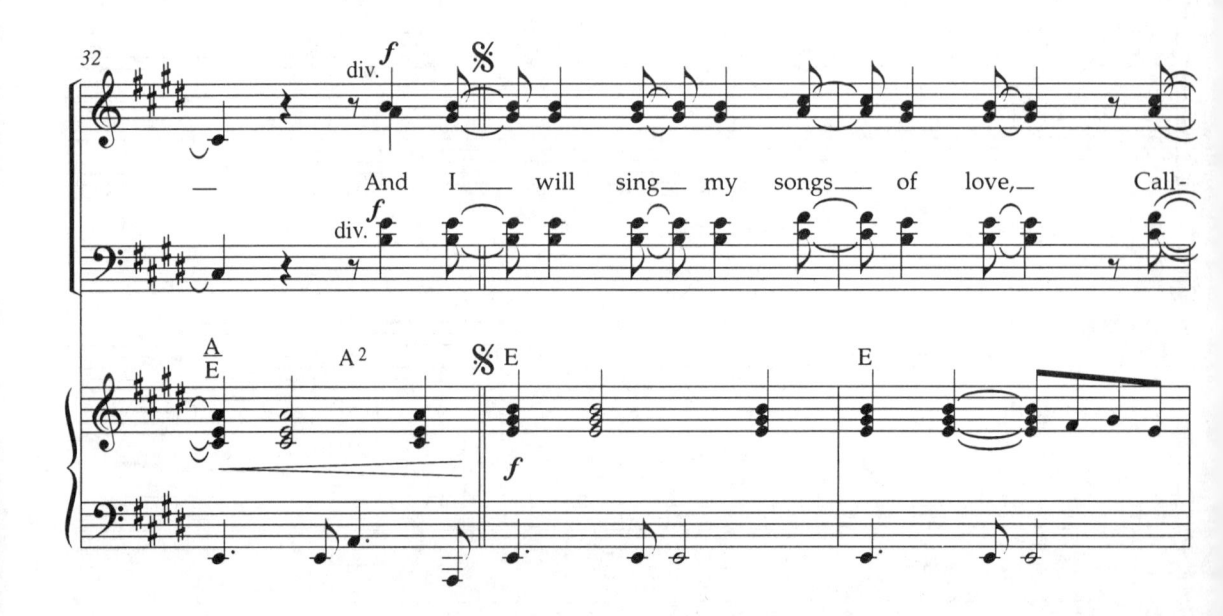

35
unis.
div.
- ing out_ a - cross_ the earth; The King_ has come, the King_
unis.
div.
F♯m7
F♯m7
E/G♯
A2
38
PRAISE TEAM
f
The King has_ come._
_ of love_ has come._
And trou-
A2
E
E

-bled minds can know His peace, Cap-tive hearts can be re-leased; The King has come, the King of love has come.

My lov-er's breath is sweet-est wine, I am His prize and He is mine; How can a sin-ner know such joy? Be-cause of

Je - sus. The wounds of love are in His hands,
MEN unis. *mf*

The price is paid for sin - ful man; Ac - cept - ed

child, for - giv - en son, Be - cause of Je - sus.

— And I — And my — desire is to have You near; Lord, You know that You are welcome here. Be-fore such love, be-fore such grace, I will let the walls come down. I will let the walls come down.

And I will sing my songs of love, Calling out across the earth; The King has come, the King

30

85

**PRAISE TEAM**
*f*

The King has come._ _of love_ has come._ And trou-bled minds_ can know_ His peace,_ Cap-tive hearts_ can be_

Bb2   F   F   F   F   Gm7

re - leased; The King has come, the King of love has come.

I will sing my songs to You, and I

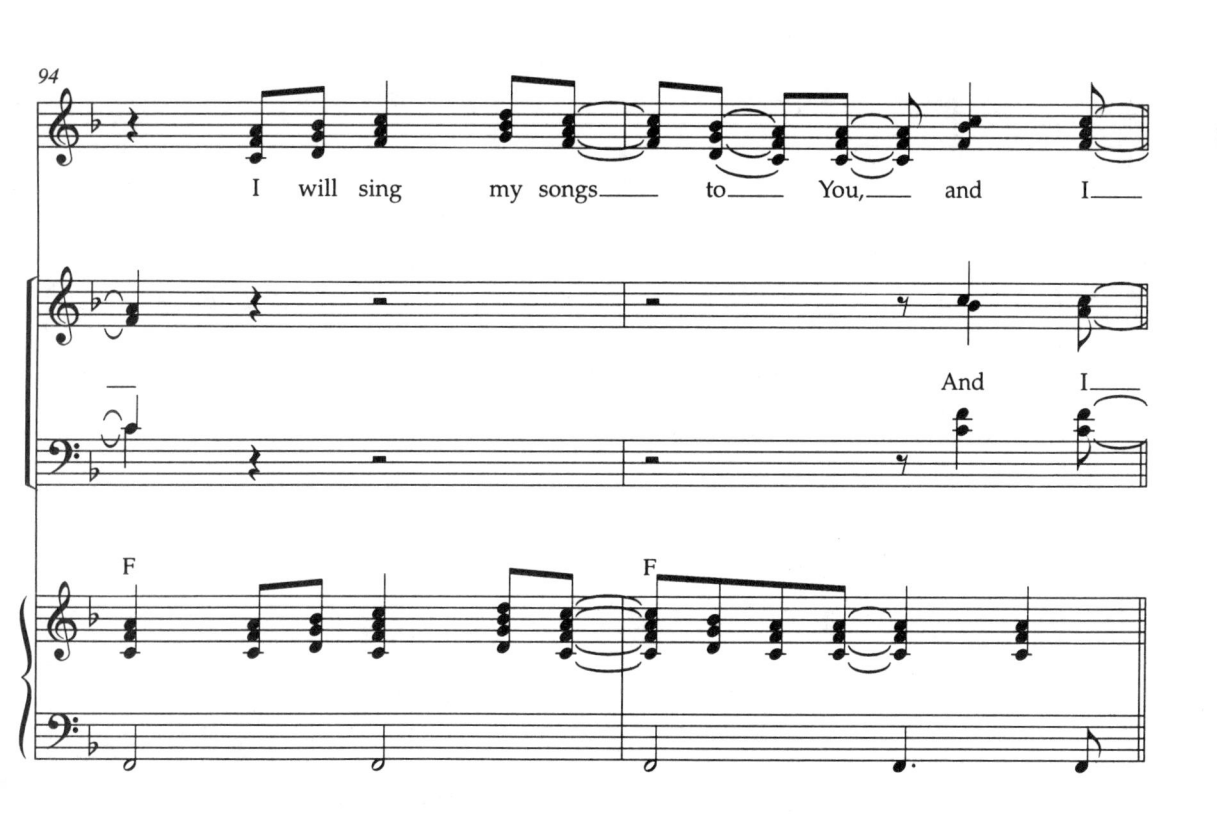

And I

96
Sing my songs.
will sing my songs of love, Call - ing out a - cross
F
F
Gm7
99
unis.
div.
the earth; The King has come, the King of love has come.
unis.
div.
Gm7
F/A
B♭2
B♭2

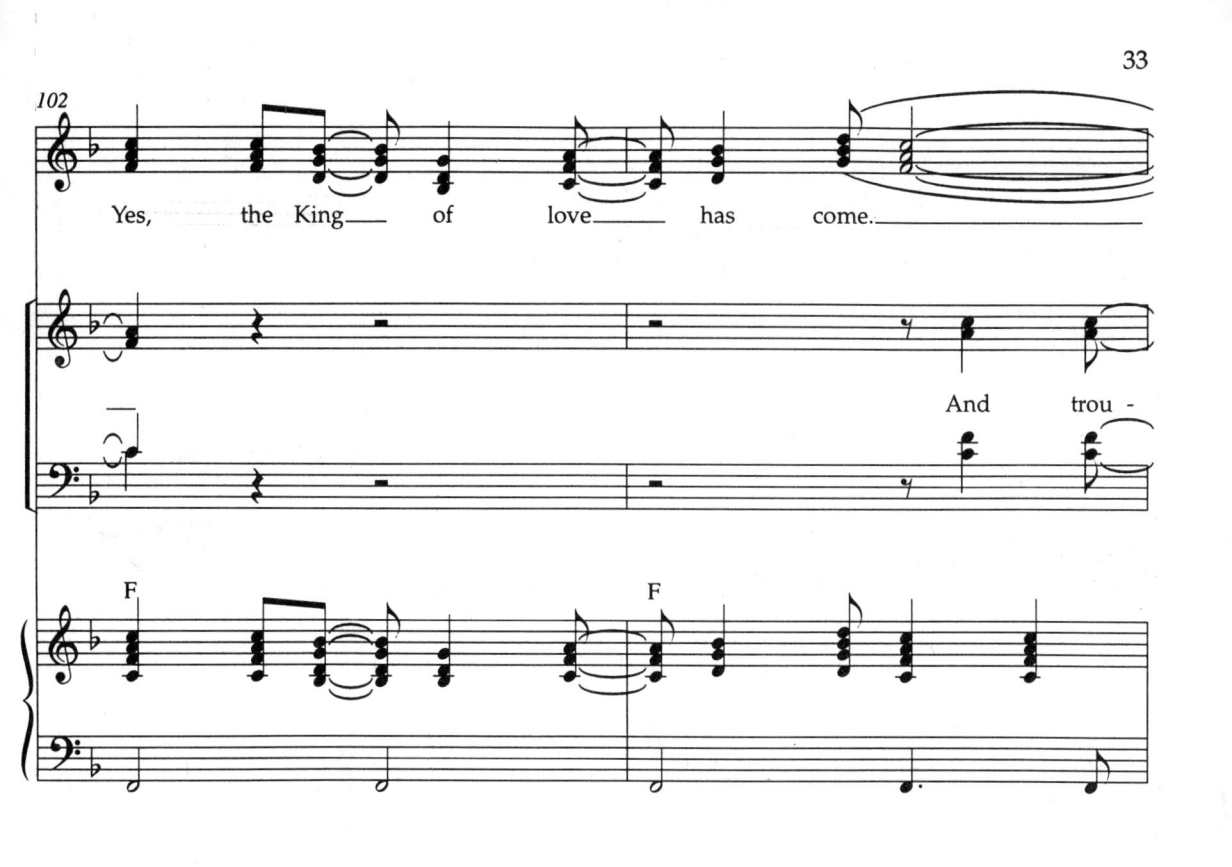

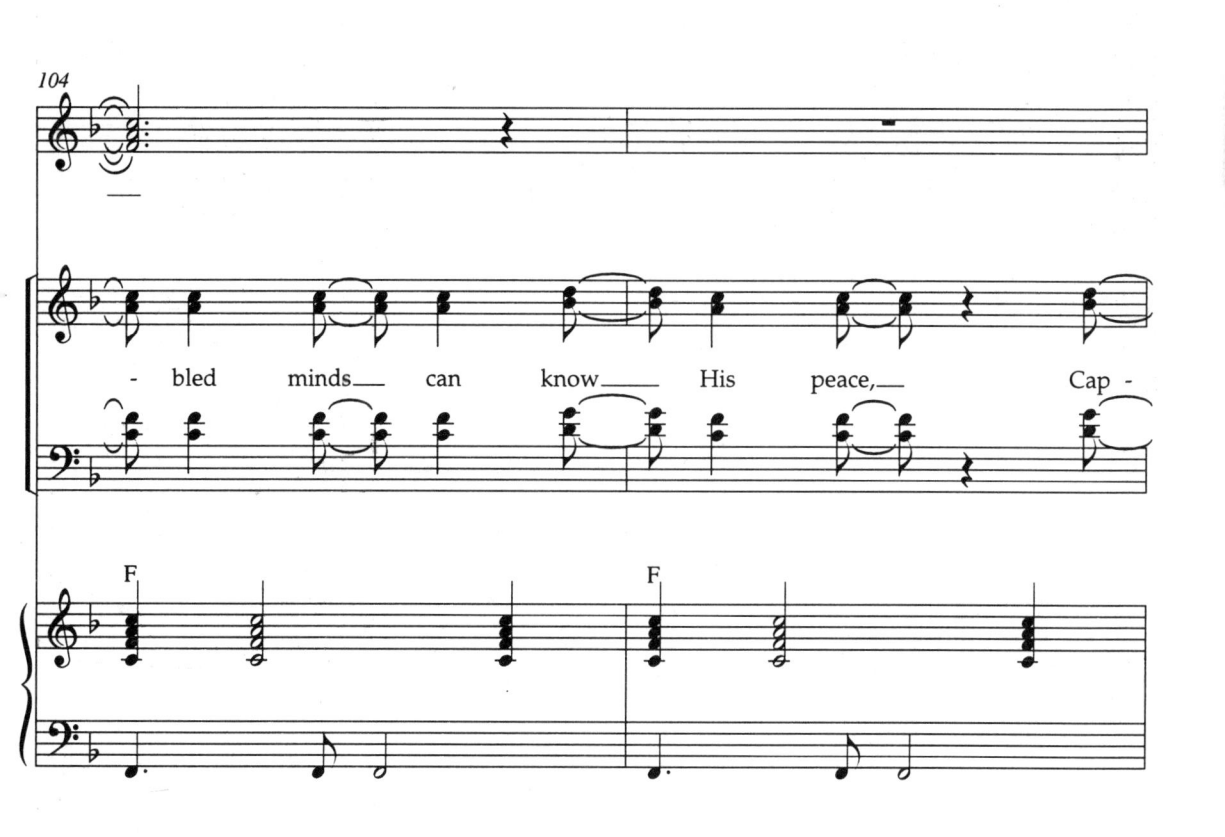

Yes, the King of love has come. And trou-bled minds can know His peace, Cap-

-tive hearts can be re-leased; The King has come, the King of love has come. The King of love has come.

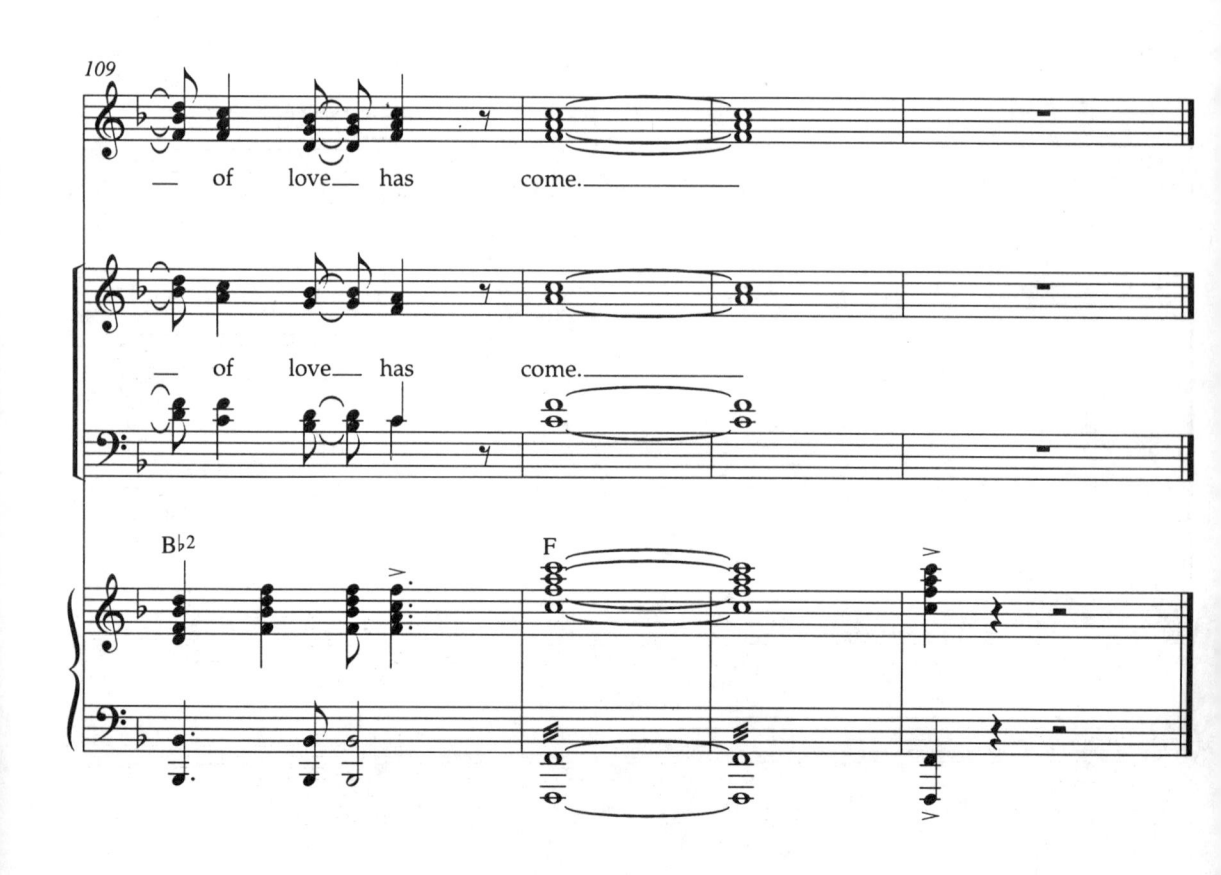

# Jesus Paid It All

ELVINA M. HALL

JOHN T. GRAPE
*Arranged by J. Daniel Smith*

hear the Savior say: "Thy strength in-deed is small. Child of weak-ness, watch and pray. Find in Me thine All in All."

21
mf
div.
Je - sus paid it all;
mf
div.
C
C sus / D
C / E
C / F
mf
23
All to Him I owe.
Em7
Am7
Dm7
Dm7 / G
25
Sin had left a crim - son stain;
He
C
C sus / D
C / E
F2
F
Am / F♯

washed_____ it white as snow.

For_____ noth - ing good have I

Where - by Thy grace to claim;

I will

36
18
wash my gar-ments white In the blood of Cal-v'ry's
Em7 Am Fm/A♭ C/G F/G
39
mf
Lamb. And when be - fore the
C A♭9 G♭/A♭ D♭6 9
41
div.
throne I stand in Him com - plete, "Je - sus
B♭m2 G♭m6/A D♭/A♭ G♭M7

died my soul to save," My lips shall still re-peat. Je-sus paid it all; All to Him I

51
owe.
Sin had left a crim - son
C
A
C♯
D
D sus
E
D
F♯
20
53
stain;
He washed it white as
G2
G
B m
G♯
D
A
G M7
A
55
snow.
Oh,
Je - sus paid it
D
C 9♭5
C 9
D
D sus
E

57
all;
All
to Him I
D
F♯
D
G
F♯m7
Bm7
59
owe.
Sin
had left a crim - son
C
A
C♯
D
D sus
E
D
F♯
61
rit.
mp
stain;
He
unis.
mp
G2
G
Bm
G♯
rit.
decresc.

washed it white as snow.

# High and Exalted

*with*
Holy Is the Lord

Words and Music by
KYLE RASMUSSEN
*Arranged by J. Daniel Smith*

† "Holy Is the Lord"
SOLO (freely)

Ho- ly, ho - ly,

† Words and Music by LYNN DeSHAZO
© Copyright 1996 and this arr. © 2001 Integrity's Hosanna! Music/ASCAP. All rights reserved. International copyright secured. Used by permission.

© Copyright 1996 and this arr. © 2001 Integrity's Hosanna! Music/ASCAP.
All rights reserved. International copyright secured. Used by permission.

ho-ly_____ is the Lord, our_____ God; Ho-ly, ho-ly, ho-ly is the Lord.

25
CHOIR
mp
Ho - ly, ho -
mp
E♭ E♭ Cm7
28
ly, ho - ly is the
Cm7 E♭/A♭ A♭ B♭7sus B♭7
31
24 2nd time
Lord, our God; Ho -
E♭/B♭ B♭7sus B♭7 E♭

ly, ho - ly, ho - ly is the Lord.

And He is wor - thy to re - ceive our

praise; And to be pro-claimed as the Lord o-ver all. all. He is wor - thy. Ho - ly, He is ho - ly, ho - ly unis. is the Lord, our God;

61
Ho - ly, He is ho -
div.
F
F
Dm7
64
molto. rit.
ly, ho - ly is the
Dm7
F/B♭
B♭
C7sus
C7
Fsus/C
molto. rit.
67
26
Driving (♩ = ca. 76)
Lord.
F
Dm7
F/B♭
f

70
CHOIR unis.
mf
He is high and ex - alt - ed and wor -
Dm7 Am7 Gm7 F/A B♭2
mf
72
- thy of praise, With our hearts we will love and a - dore;
Dm7 C B♭2 F2/A
74
He is high and ex - alt - ed and wor -
C F2/A B♭2
76
27
- thy of praise, Ho - ly is the Lord.
Dm7 C B♭2 C

52

-thy of praise, Holy is the Lord. Holy, holy, holy is the Lord;

Holy, holy, holy is the Lord. He is high and exalted and worthy of praise, With our hearts we will love and adore;

*If tessitura is too high, all men may sing bass part (melody) to measure 109. Ladies may divide, with altos singing cued notes.

-thy of praise, With our hearts we will love and adore;

He is high and exalted and wor-

-thy of praise, Holy is the Lord.

57

# How Deep the Father's Love for Us

*With deep gratitude*  (♩ = ca. 84)

Near the Cross (William H. Doane)

Words and Music by
STUART TOWNEND
Arranged by J. Daniel Smith

18
unis. mp
How
unis. mp
D4/2
D
D4/2
21
deep the Fa - ther's love for us, how
D
Em7
D/F♯
G2
24
div.
unis.
vast be - yond all mea - sure; That
D/A
Bm7
A7sus
A7

60

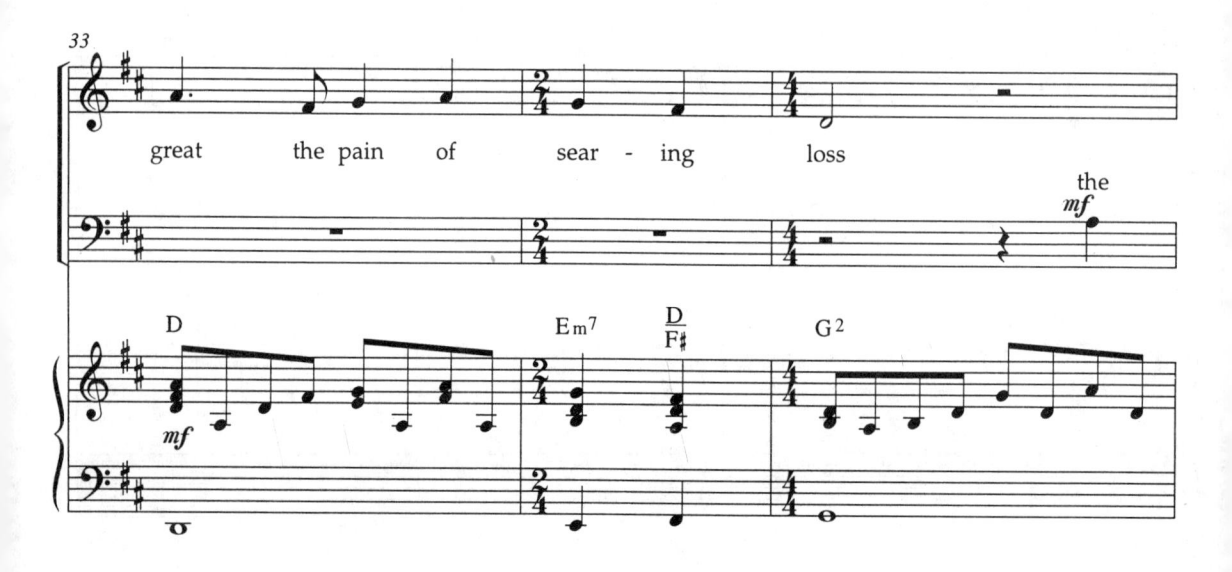

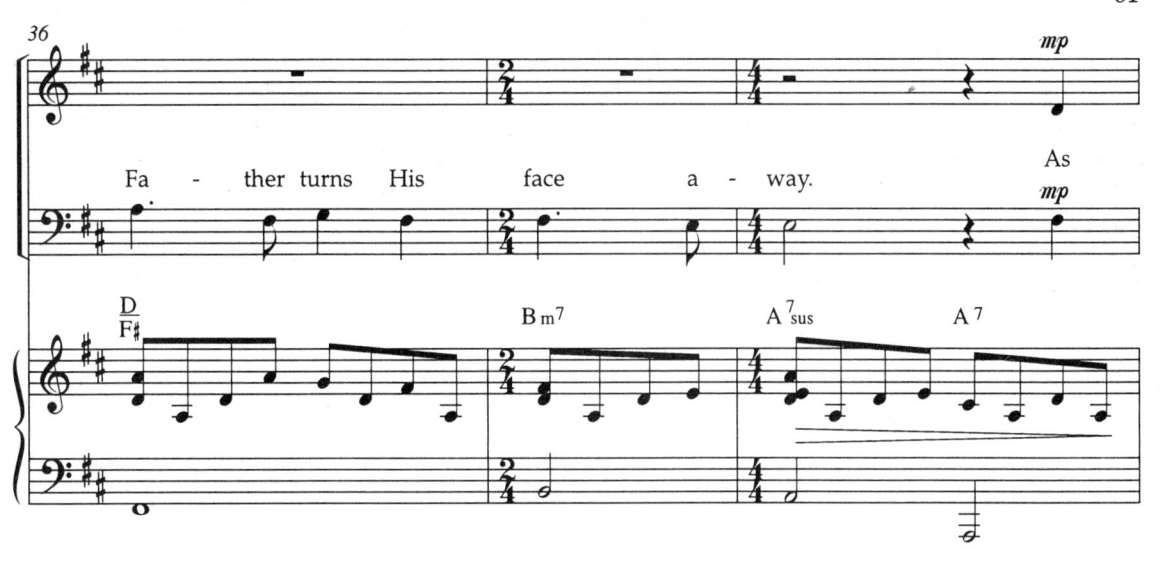

Father turns His face away. As wounds which mar the Chosen One bring many sons to glory.

Be - hold the Man up - on a cross, my sin up - on His shoul -

ders; A-shamed, I hear my mock-ing voice call out a-mong the scoff-ers. It was my sin that held Him

there un- til it was ac- com- plished; His dy- ing breath has brought me life, I know that it is finished.

I will not boast in any-

84
thing, no gifts, no pow'r, no wis -
B♭2
F/C
Dm
87
dom; But I will boast in Je - sus
C7sus
C7
F
Gm7
F/A
90
Christ, His death and res - ur - rec -
B♭2
F/C
C7sus
C7

tion. Why should I gain from His re-
ward? I can-not give an an-
swer. But this I know with all my

heart; His wounds have paid my ran-som. Why should I gain from His re-ward? I can-not give an an-

111
mp
swer. But this I know with all my
unis.
C7sus C7 F Gm7 F/A
114
rit.
heart; His wounds have paid my ran -
B♭2 F/C C7sus C7
117
unis. p
Slower
som. But this I know with all my
F F Gm7 F/A

heart; His wounds have paid my ran - som.

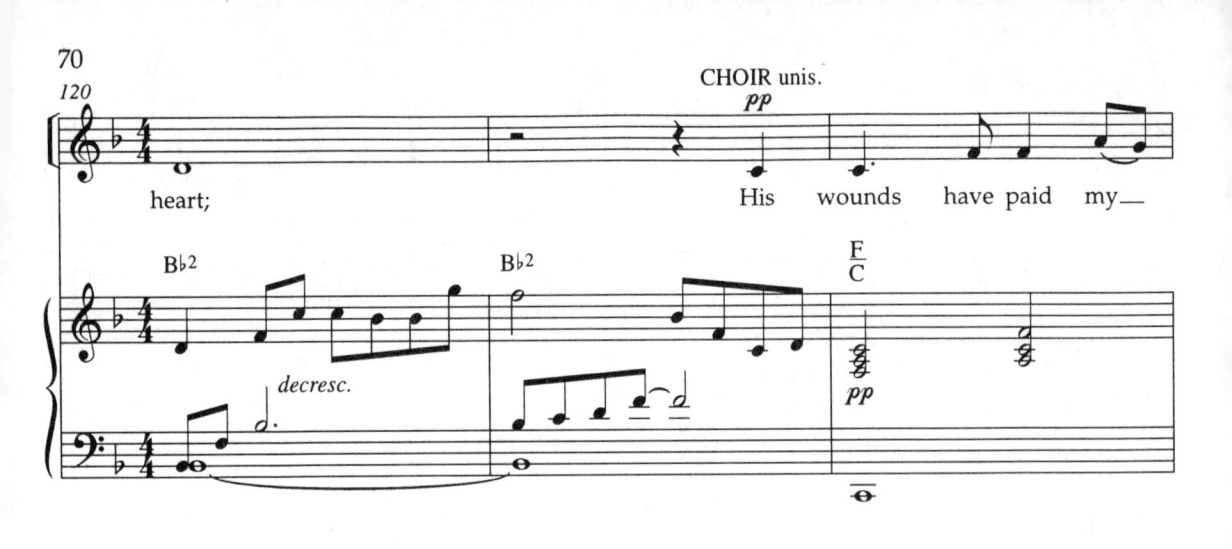

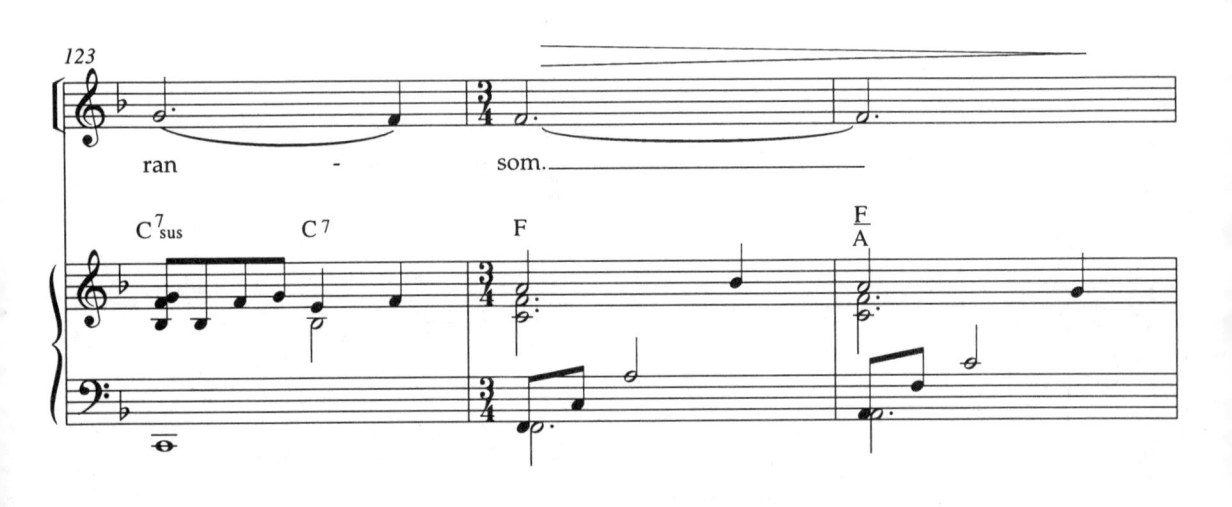

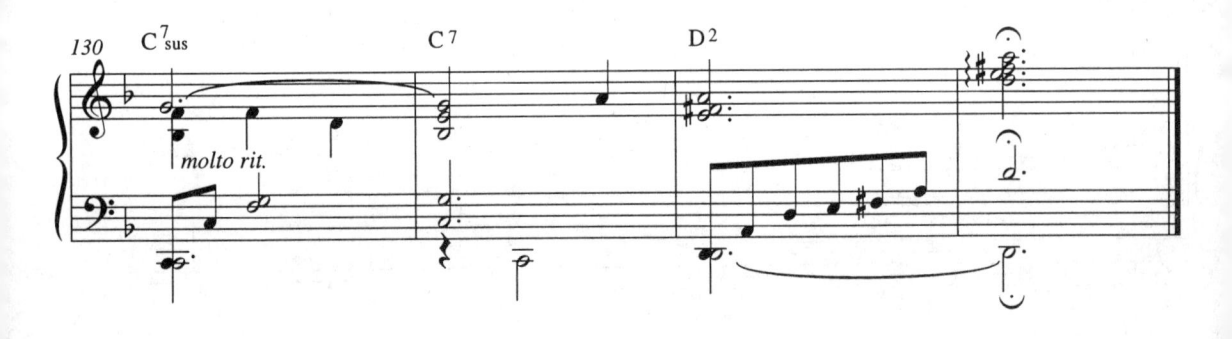

# At Calvary

WILLIAM R. NEWELL
*Aggressively* (♩ = ca. 86)

DANIEL B. TOWNER
*Arranged by J. Daniel Smith*

© Copyright 2001 Broadman Press / SESAC. Nashville, TN 37234.

12
ty and pride, Car - ing not my Lord was
B♭2
F/A
14
cru - ci - fied, Know - ing not it was for
E♭M7/G
E♭m6/F
B♭2/F
E♭M7
16
35
me He died on Cal - va - ry.
Dm7
Gm7
Cm7
F9
B♭
B♭4 2/C
C♯°7
B♭/D

Mer - cy there was great and grace was free;

Par - don there was mul - ti - plied to me;

There my bur - dened soul found lib - er - ty, at

Cal - va - ry.

LADIES unis.
By God's Word at last my sin I learned; Then I trem-bled at the law I'd spurned,

Till my guilty soul imploring turned to Calvary.

Now I've giv'n to Jesus ev'rything;

Now I gladly own Him as my King;

Now my rap-tured soul can on-ly sing of Cal-va-ry.

Mer-cy there was great and grace was free;

Par - don there was mul-ti-plied to me;

There my bur-dened soul found lib - er - ty, at

Cal - va - ry.

78

O the might-y gulf that God did span at Cal-va-ry! Mer-cy there was great and grace was free; Par-don there was multiplied to me; There my bur-dened soul found liberty, at Cal-va-ry. Mer-cy there was great and grace was free;

Pardon there was multiplied to me;
There my burdened soul found liberty, at
Calvary. At Calva-

ry. Mer-cy there was great at Cal - va -

ry,_____ Cal - va -

ry.

# You Are Holy

Words and Music by
REUBEN MORGAN
Arranged by J. Daniel Smith

Lord, there is none_ like_ You._ You are ho-ly,_ ho-ly;_ Glo-ry to You_ a-lone._

15
p
You are ho - ly, ho - ly;
p
A2
Am/E
E
p
F♯m/D♯
G♯♯9/♯5
C♯m2
C♯m
18
Lord, there is none like You. You are
F♯m7
E
DM7
F♯m7/B
20
ho - ly, ho - ly; Glo-ry to You a-lone.
44
Am/E
E
F♯m/D♯
G♯♯9/♯5
C♯m2
F♯m7
F♯m7/B

86

I'll sing Your prais - es for - ev -
er;___ Deep - er in love___ with You.___
Here in Your courts___ where I'm close___

45
unis.
to Your throne,
I've found where I be - long.
A2/C♯ Am/C E/B B7sus
div. mf
I'll sing Your prais - es for - ev -
E A/B E EM7
- er;
Deep - er in love with You.
AM7 F♯m/A E2/G♯ F♯m7

35
div.
Here in Your courts where I'm close
div.
B7sus
B7
E
E/D
46
37
unis.
decresc.
to Your throne,
unis.
I've found where I be-long.
decresc.
A2/C♯
Am/C
E/B
B7sus
D6/9
decresc.
40
p
You are ho - ly, ho - ly;
p
D6/9
Am/E
E
F♯m/D♯
G♯♯9♯5
C♯m2
C♯m
p

43
Lord, there is none like You. You are
F♯m7 E D M7 F♯m7/B
45
ho - ly, ho - ly;
Am/E E F♯m/D♯ G♯♯9♯5 C♯m2
47
47
Glo - ry to You a - lone.
F♯m7 F♯m7/B E A/B

49
mf
div.
I'll sing Your prais - es for - ev - er;
mf
div.
unis.
E
E M7
A M7
F♯m/A
E2/G♯
mf
51
unis.
Deep - er in love with You.
F♯m7
B7sus
B7
53
div.
Here in Your courts where I'm close to Your throne,
div.
unis.
E
E/D
A2/C♯
Am/C

I've found where I belong.

I'll sing Your praises forever;

Deeper in love with You.

61
div.
Here in Your courts where I'm close to Your throne,
div.
unis.
F
F/E♭
B♭2/D
B♭m/D♭
49
63
unis.
I've found where I be - long.
F/C
C7sus
F
B♭/C
65
div.
I'll sing Your prais - es for - ev - er;
div.
unis.
F
F M7
B♭M7
B♭6
F2/A

Deep - er in love___ with___ You.___

Here in Your courts___ where I'm close___ to Your throne,___

I've found where I___ be-long.___

Slower (♩ = ca. 60)
74
rit.
div.
mp
Here in Your courts where I'm close
mp
Gm7/4
B♭6/C
F
F/E♭
rit.
77
unis.
rit.
to Your throne,
I've found where I be - long.
B♭2/D
B♭m/D♭
F/C
C7sus
rit.
79
N.C.
E♭6/9
F2
p
pp

# The Father's Song

Words and Music by
MATT REDMAN
Arranged by J. Daniel Smith

With warmth (♩ = ca. 98)

*I have heard so many songs, listened to a thousand tongues; But*

13
there is one that sounds a - bove them all.
Em9
GM7/A
A13
15
The Fa-ther's song, the
Bm2
A/C♯
G2
D2
18
Fa-ther's love, You sang it o - ver me and for e -
DM7/C♯
D/C
G2/B
21
51
ter-ni-ty It's writ-ten on my heart.
Em9
GM7/A
A13
D
G/D
DM7

97

31
div.
song.
Heav - en's per - fect
div.
Bm2
A
C♯
D
33
unis.
mys - ter - y,
the King of Love has
GM7
B
A2
C♯
35
sent for me;
And now You're sing - ing
sent for me;
unis.
D2
F♯
G2

o - ver me

the Fa - ther's song.

I have heard so man-y songs,

lis-tened to a thou - sand tongues; But there is one that

sounds a-bove them all.

The Fa-ther's song, the Fa-ther's love, You sang it o - ver me and for e - ter-ni-ty It's writ-ten on my heart. Heav-en's per-fect mel-o-dy, the Cre-a-tor's sym-pho-ny; You are sing-ing o-ver me the Fa-ther's song.

64
div.
Heav - en's per - fect mys - ter - y,
div.
B♭/D
E♭
A♭M7/C
66
unis.
the King of Love has sent for me;
sent for
unis.
B♭2/D
E♭2/G
68
And now You're sing - ing o - ver me
me;
A♭2
Fm7

70
the Fa - ther's song.
Bb7sus
Bb7
Eb
cresc.
Eb
73
54
molto rit.
AbM7
C
Bb2
D
C
E
molto rit.
76
div.
f
Heav-en's per-fect mys-ter - y,
a tempo
unis.
the King of Love has
F
F
A
BbM7
D
C2
E
a tempo

79
mp
sent for me;
And now You're sing-ing o-ver me
sent for me;
unis.
F2
A
B♭2
Gm7
mp
82
the Fa - ther's song.
mp
Csus
C
F
F
decresc.
85
p
The Fa-ther's song, the Fa-ther's love, You sang it o - ver
me.
p
F2
FM7
E
F
E♭
p

me and for e-ter-ni-ty It's writ-ten on my heart.

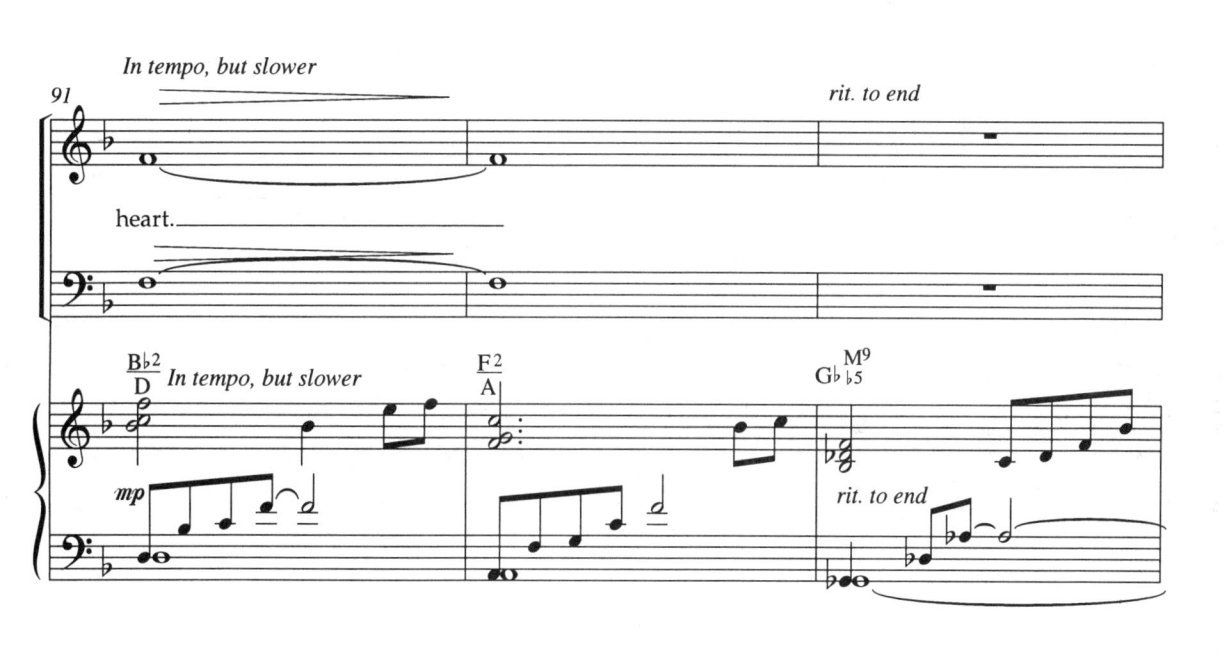

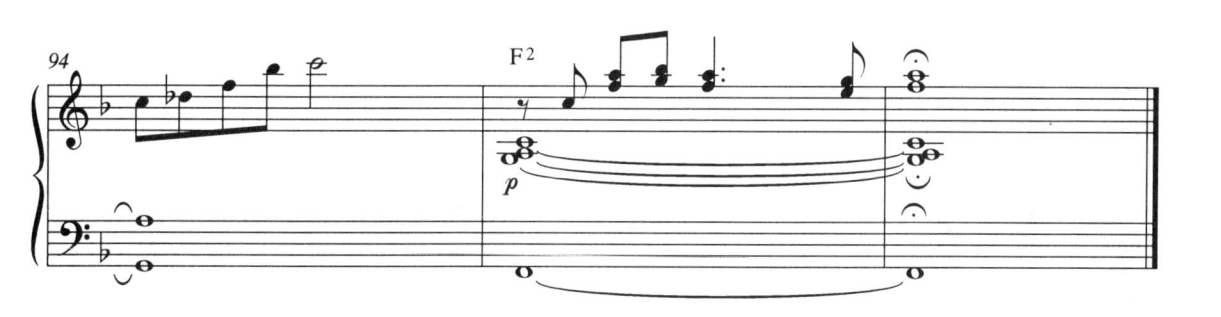

# The Wonders of God

Words and Music by
RICK MUCHOW
Arranged by J. Daniel Smith

Celebrative (♩ = ca. 100)

*sing a-bout the great-ness of the Fa-ther;— Let's*

© Copyright 1992 and this arr. © 2001 Encouraging Music.
All rights reserved. Used by permission.

sing a-bout the glo-ry of His Son; And the
Ho-ly Spir-it dwell-ing a-mong us; Let's
sing a-bout the won-ders of God, Oh,

13
unis.
let's sing a-bout the won-ders of God,
unis.
E♭ B♭/D Cm7 F♯°7
56
15
div.
unis.
Oh, let's
div.
unis.
Gm F E♭ B♭/D
17
sing a-bout the won-ders of God. Let's
Cm7 Fsus B♭2 A♭2 E♭2

sing about the greatness of the Father; Let's sing about the glory of His Son; And the Holy Spirit dwelling among us; Let's

25
div.
sing a-bout the won-ders of God,
Oh,
div.
B♭/D
E♭
F♯°7
Gm
F
27
unis.
let's sing a-bout the won-ders of God,
unis.
E♭
B♭/D
Cm7
F♯°7
57
1st time
2nd time to Coda
29
div.
unis.
Oh,
let's
div.
unis.
Gm
F
E♭
B♭/D
2nd time to Coda

sing a-bout the won-ders of God. The

earth and heav-en a-bove

Ech-o the won-ders of His love.

112

The earth and heav-en a-bove

Ech-o the won-ders of His

49
div.
mf
love.
Join the cho - rus: God is for us, the
div.
G sus
G♯°7
A m
C/G
F M7
C/E
60
52
cresc.
great - ness won - der of all,
of
f
cresc.
D m7
E m7
F
G7sus
54
unis.
all.
Let's sing a - bout the great - ness of the
unis.
G7
C2
G sus/F

115

Father;— Let's sing about— the glory of His Son;— And the Holy Spirit dwelling among— us; Let's sing about— the wonders of God,—

62
div.
unis.
Oh,
let's
div.
unis.
Am
G
F
C
E
64
div.
sing a - bout the won - ders of God,
Oh,
div.
Dm7
G#°7
Am
G
66
unis.
let's sing a - bout the won - ders of
unis.
F
C
E
Dm7
G sus

117

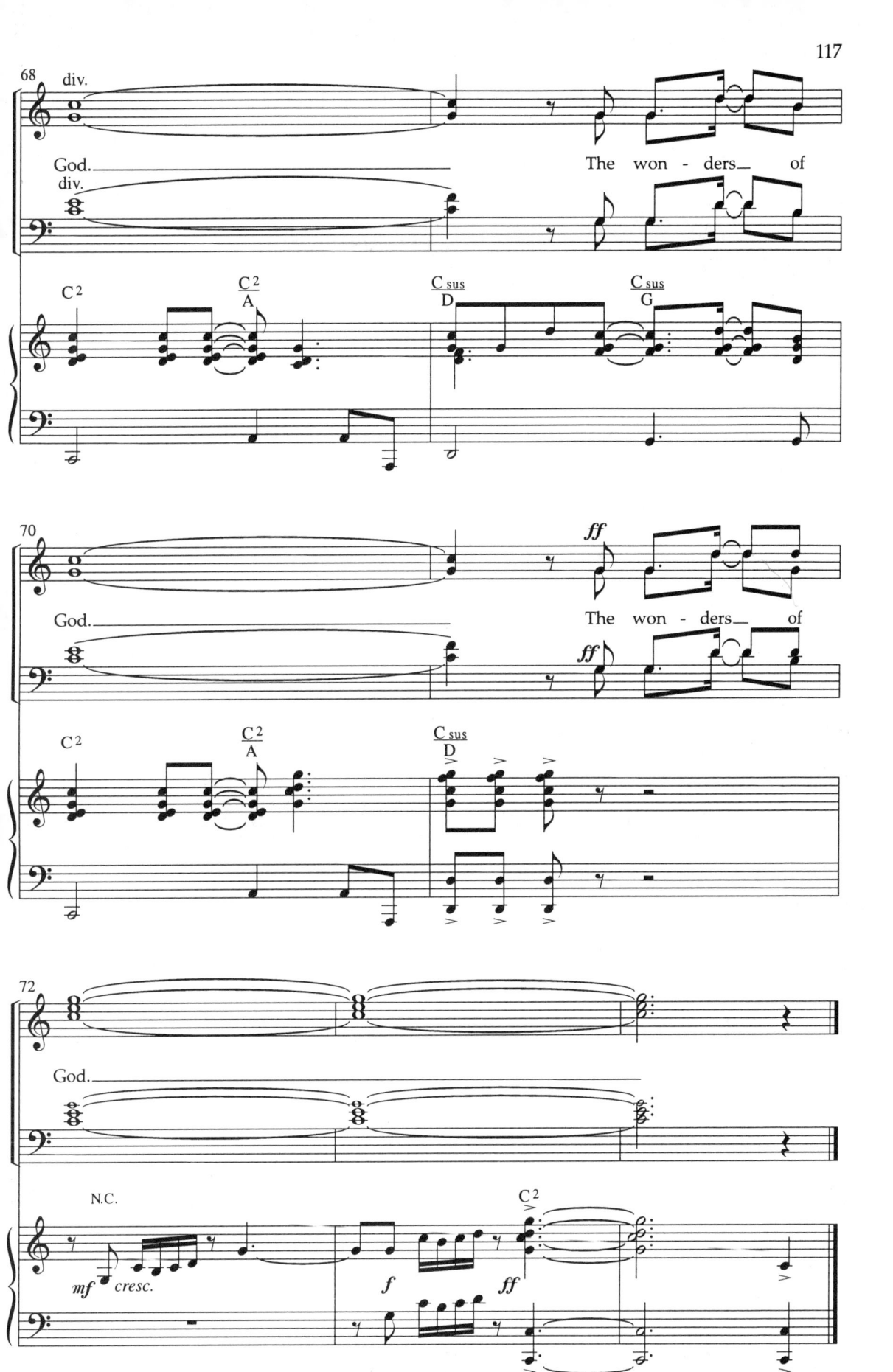

# O Lord, You're Beautiful

Words and Music by
KEITH GREEN
Arranged by J. Daniel Smith

© Copyright 1980 and this arr. © 2001 Birdwing Music/BMG Songs, Inc.
(All print rights controlled by EMI Christian Music Publishing). Used by permission.

1st time: LADIES unis.
2nd time: CHOIR unis.
mp
16
O Lord, You're beau - ti -
D2 D G/D D
19
ful, Your face is
A/C♯ A sus/B A A/G D/F♯
22
all I seek, For
G D/F♯ A A
25
when Your eyes are on this
Bm2 Bm F♯/A♯ Bm/A

63 1st time
64 2nd time
28
child, Your grace a - bounds to
Bm/G♯ Em7 D/G A7sus A7
31
1
CHOIR unis.
mp
2
me. O me.
Dsus D Dsus
34
SOLO
mp
I want to take Your Word and
D Dsus/E D/F♯ G D/F♯ Em Bm/D
37
3
shine it all a - round, But first help me
A/C♯ A D Em7 D/F♯

just to live it, Lord.

And when I'm do-ing well, help me to never seek a crown, For my reward is giv-ing glo-ry to You.

O Lord, please light the fire That once burned bright and clear; Re-place the lamp of my first

62
66
love That burns with ho - ly
Gm/E
Cm7
Bb/Eb
F7sus
F7
65
fear.
I want to take Your
unis.
mf
Bbsus
Bb
Bbsus/C
Bb/D
Eb
Bb/D
68
div.
3
Word and shine it all a-round, But first help me
div.
Cm
Gm/Bb
F/A
F
Bb
Cm7
Bb/D

just to live it, Lord.

And when I'm doing well, help me to never seek a crown, For my reward is giving

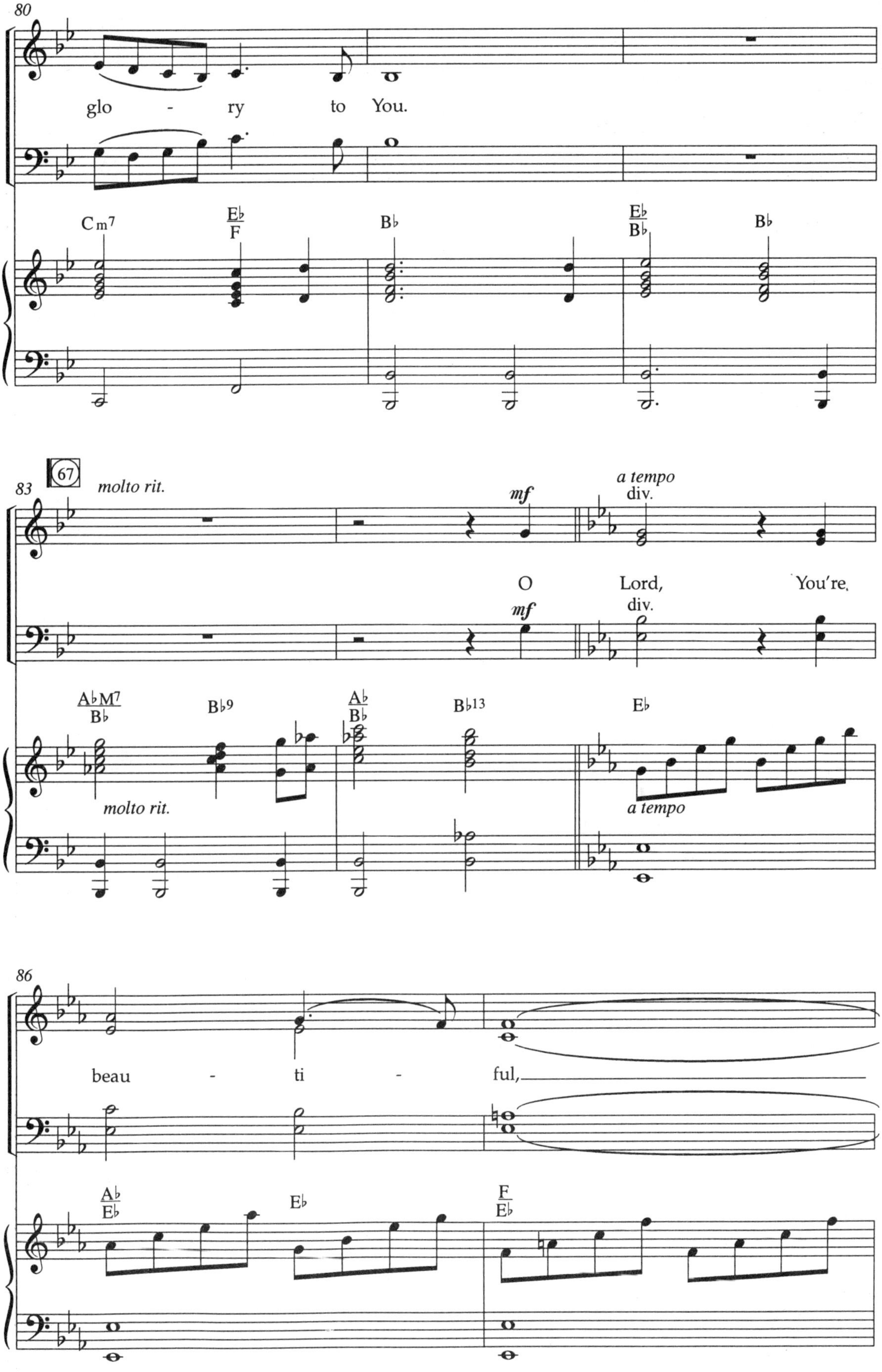
80
glo - ry to You.
Cm7
Eb/F
Bb
Eb/Bb
Bb
67
83
molto rit.
mf
a tempo
div.
O Lord, You're
AbM7/Bb
Bb9
Ab/Bb
Bb13
Eb
86
beau - ti - ful,
Ab/Eb
Eb
F/Eb

126

grace a-bounds _____ to me.

O Lord, You're beau-ti-ful, Your face is

all I seek, For when Your eyes are on this child, Your grace abounds to me.